Praise for
The Spirituality That Heals
by Michael Youssef

"Michael Youssef leads us out of the shadowlands of superficial spirituality into the promised land of genuine sanctifying spirituality. Prepare to be challenged and changed!"

—HANK HANEGRAAFF, host of the *Bible Answer Man*
radio program and author of *The Prayer of Jesus*

"In a broken, hurting world that longs for hope, Michael Youssef has provided a remedy for our souls that is both biblical and practical. Read this and embrace the healing power of God."

—DR. JOSEPH M. STOWELL, president of Moody Bible Institute

"Michael Youssef is one of the most gifted pastors of our generation. I recommend *The Spirituality That Heals* to all who seek the healing power of Jesus Christ."

—LARRY BURKETT, author of *Nothing to Fear: The Key to Cancer Survival* and chairman of the board of Crown Financial Ministries

"Michael Youssef does an inspiring job of teaching the remarkable truth about the work of the Holy Spirit. His book will invite you to empty yourself and seek to be filled with God's Spirit."

—NICKY CRUZ, international evangelist and author of *One Holy Fire* and *Run, Baby, Run*

HEAL

Me,

O GOD

HEAL

Me,

O GOD

Yielding to His Touch
in Your Private Worship

MICHAEL YOUSSEF, PH.D.

WATERBROOK
PRESS

HEAL ME, O GOD
PUBLISHED BY WATERBROOK PRESS
2375 Telstar Drive, Suite 160
Colorado Springs, Colorado 80920
A division of Random House, Inc.

ISBN 1-57856-558-8

Library of Congress Cataloging-in-Publication Data
  Youssef, Michael.
     Heal me, o God : yielding to His touch in your private worship /
  by Michael Youssef.— 1st ed.
       p. cm.
       ISBN 1-57856-558-8
    1. Spirituality. 2. Healing—Religious aspects—Christianity. I. Title.
    BV4509.5.Y675 2003
    234'.13—dc21

                                                           2003006167

Printed in the United States of America
2003—First Edition

10 9 8 7 6 5 4 3 2 1

CONTENTS

ACKNOWLEDGMENTS

The more books I write, the more I find myself dependent on the help of others. I am of course thankful to Ron Lee and his crew at WaterBrook Press. But my deepest indebtedness goes to my very able and gifted research and writing assistant, Marya Lewis. Her commitment to excellence and attention to the details—while at the same time striving to preserve the heart of what I want to communicate—is truly unique.

The fruit of the Spirit is love, joy,
peace, patience, kindness, goodness,
faithfulness, gentleness and self-control.
Against such things there is no law.

GALATIANS 5:22–23

THE HEALING TOUCH OF GOD

Intuitively, we all sense that we are not whole physically, emotionally, or spiritually. And we possess within us a deep need to be made whole. Given the fundamental nature of this human need, it is not surprising that healing and spirituality have become the Siamese twins of our modern world.

Perhaps this is because we have come to realize that technology alone cannot solve our problems, especially in matters of the body, the mind, and the spirit. Time after time, men and women suffering from life-threatening illnesses are told by the best minds in healthcare, "We've done all that medical science can do. I'm sorry, but we can't help you." Deep inside we wonder if there is something in the unseen world that can bring us to greater wholeness in this life and in the life to come.

The longing for healing and wholeness has set many on a quest for spirituality. This quest stretches from transcendental meditation to stress management to seeking out the services of a wide array of faith healers—leading many into what I call "shadow spirituality."

We see evidence of this in a variety of forms. A University of Chicago poll revealed that 67 percent of Americans believe in the supernatural, and 42 percent said they have had contact with the dead.[1] Another source claimed that sixty million Americans, in one way or another, are involved in the New Age movement.[2]

But that only begins to tell the story. One out of four Americans say they believe in reincarnation.[3] Forty million Americans depend on astrology, with a billion or more people worldwide looking to the stars for guidance.[4] In addition, more than one hundred thousand Americans are registered as witches or warlocks.[5] So widespread is the interest in all forms of spirituality that *Forbes* magazine estimated the New Age movement had created a 3.5 billion dollar market![6]

But humanity, with its intense longing for wholeness, must be directed to the only *true* spirituality, the spirituality that is

1. John Naisbitt and Patricia Aburdene, *Megatrends 2000: Ten New Directions for the 1990's* (New York: Morrow, 1990), 293.

2. Christopher Blake, "New Age, Old Myths," *Message,* November 1989, 6-7.

3. John Dart, "New Age Ideas and Theological Vacuum: Can Churches Resist the Pull of Paranormal?" *Los Angeles Times,* 14 February 1987, 114-5.

4. Alan Bunce, "Searching for Secrets in the Stars," *Christian Science Monitor,* 5-6 July 1988, 1-2.

5. Dave Bass, "Drawing Down the Moon," *Christianity Today,* 29 April 1991, 14-9.

6. Mike Oppenheimer, "The New Age Movement," *Forbes,* June 1987.

rooted in a daily relationship with God through His Holy Spirit. That relationship can be secured only through the acceptance of Jesus Christ's death as the payment of the debt for our sin. In His Word, God gives us a clear standard for what it means to pursue the spirituality that brings genuine healing. The more we understand God's plan for developing biblical spirituality, the more we will experience the wholeness that He alone can bring.

The focused, thirty-one-day format of this book is designed to guide you in a daily, personal time of worshiping the Lord. As you read, study, and pray, you will put yourself in a position to experience God's healing presence through the manifestation of the fruit of the Holy Spirit.

I pray that, as you spend time with the Lord through this daily exercise, you will experience His amazing love, the guidance of His Spirit, and the assurance that comes from a personal relationship with His Son, Jesus Christ. Truly, there can be no lasting peace apart from knowing Jesus Christ as Savior and Lord of all. Hence, there is only one spiritual path that leads to true peace and healing.

May God meet with you and bless you, and may your heart be opened to His truth as you begin the journey toward true spirituality—the only spirituality that will make you whole.

This is good, and pleases God our Savior, who wants all men to be saved and to come to a knowledge of the truth. For there is one God and one mediator between God and men, the man Christ Jesus. (1 Timothy 2:3-5)

PART I

THE SOURCE
OF TRUE SPIRITUALITY

I will ask the Father, and he will
give you another Counselor to be
with you forever—the Spirit of truth.

JOHN 14:16-17

EXPOSING
"SHADOW SPIRITUALITY"

Look around and you'll be amazed at all the manifestations of the "self" movement, including self-actualization, self-empowerment, and self-improvement. It is as if all the answers to your problems are to be found by looking within.

But this is spirituality only in the loosest sense. In truth, it is "shadow spirituality"—merely a shadow of the real thing. Shadow spirituality asks individuals to look inward, to put themselves at the center of the universe while pushing God so far to the fringes that He is left out of the picture. What remains is a spirituality of self.

In other words, shadow spirituality replaces the God of the universe with the "god within." This god is not the triune God revealed in the Bible, but rather a force that supposedly compels a person to improve himself. This god is nothing more than the human ability to learn, grow, and develop—all of which are God's gifts to people. None of these abilities, however, is capable of regenerating the human heart. Only God has that power.

The ascendance of shadow spirituality has influenced even traditional churches, and two great heresies have resulted. One is the heresy that all spirituality is good spirituality. The second is the heresy that all religions are valid as long as they promote peace and unity. Don't allow false teachers to mislead you. Instead, lay hold of the *only* form of spiritual power that genuinely heals you and makes you whole. It is only in God's true spirituality that you find solace for your heart's deepest longings—healing for the soul, peace for the mind, and comfort for broken emotions. This healing comes only when you are committed to the pursuit of God's true spirituality.

The Holy Spirit is calling you to look upward, to put God at the center of all that you will face today, and to grow in understanding and in relationship with Him. Will you invite the Holy Spirit to fill you afresh this day? God has promised that He will reveal Himself to you if you truly seek Him with all your heart.

———◆———

Lord, I want to seek You and Your true spirituality. Your Word says that "a natural man does not accept the things of the Spirit of God, for they are foolishness to him; and he cannot understand them, because they are spiritually appraised." 1 Corinthians 2:14 (NASB)

Help me to move away from falsehood and toward Your truth.

Lord, You have told us, "Then you will call upon me and come and pray to me, and I will listen to you." You have also promised, "You will seek me and find me when you seek me with all your heart." Jeremiah 29:12-13

Please, starting today, help me seek You with my entire being.

PURSUING TRUE SPIRITUALITY

The true spirituality that heals us is rooted in the fact that God is transcendent. He stands outside and apart from His creation. God is holy and just, and He is sovereign over all that He has created. He is the omnipotent, omniscient, omnipresent One who loves us unconditionally and who desires fellowship with all humankind. But He relates to us on His terms, not on ours.

Therefore, we experience true spirituality only through God's Spirit, who indwells a person as he or she responds in faith to Jesus Christ as Savior and Lord. This is the exact opposite of shadow spirituality, which contends that the "god within" merely needs to be awakened and coaxed into actualizing activities. When the superficial, feel-good emotions are stripped away, though, one quickly realizes that New Age thinking is not new at all. It is the oldest of all philosophies, dating back to the Garden of Eden, where the first man and woman thought they could be like God. Indeed, they sought to be God.

True spirituality shows us the tragic consequences of this path. All of us are born with a missing dimension caused by the sin of wanting to live independently of God. This sin separates us from Him. The only way to fill that void is through repentance of sin, faith in Jesus Christ, and the indwelling power of God's Spirit. This is the spirituality that makes us whole.

It is only when God's Spirit opens our blind spiritual eyes that we truly begin to understand ourselves and recognize our own darkness and moral corruption—in other words, our sinfulness. True spirituality helps us recognize that our desperate inner longing is not a need for independence, but rather a consuming need for dependence—dependence on the Savior.

Biblical spirituality leads us to know the light of the world, Jesus Christ, and makes it possible for us to experience wholeness of body, mind, and spirit in becoming like Him. This healing comes only as the Holy Spirit of God is invited to do His ongoing work of transformation in our lives. We are made whole when we reflect the "character-likeness" of Jesus Christ.

Will you ask the Lord to reveal to you the true answer to your inner longing, and to help you understand that your heart is made whole the moment you receive Jesus as the Savior of your soul? Will you ask God to help you walk in the light of His Son through all of life's challenges that you are facing?

———◆———

Lord, because of Your great love for me, You, who are rich in mercy, "made us alive with Christ even when we were dead in transgressions." Ephesians 2:5

Jesus revealed the source of true spirituality by saying, "I am the light of the world. Whoever follows me will never walk in darkness, but will have the light of life." John 8:12

Dear Father, thank You for sending the light of the world, Jesus.

THE SOURCE
OF TRUE SPIRITUALITY

Those who believe that true spirituality is defined exclusively by the Bible are often accused of being intolerant. I am glad to accept this false accusation as long as I am declaring the truth of God's Word, which shows us that the only source of true spirituality is the Holy Spirit.

The Bible tells us the Holy Spirit is a Person (see John 14:26; 16:13-15). He is the third member of the Trinity. The Holy Spirit is not an impersonal force; He is more aptly referred to as the Holy Spirit of almighty God.

The Hebrew word for "spirit" is *ruach,* which means "breath" or "wind." One of the foremost word pictures of the Holy Spirit found in Scripture is the title Breath of God. In fact, the first word picture associated with the Spirit is that of breath—of something that makes the air move, even to the point of vigorous or violent motion. It's a picture of energy released, an outward moving force of power.

As we seek to gain understanding of God's Spirit, it is important to know that the Holy Spirit desires God's best for us. He works in us individually. He convicts us of sin, glorifies Christ, leads and guides us, teaches and commands, intercedes for us, and provides divine help and care. The Holy Spirit prays through us that God's perfect will might be done in our lives.

In John 14–16, Jesus made it clear that after His resurrection, the Holy Spirit would be His personal representative on earth. No one else is Jesus' representative—no bishop, minister, teacher, or televangelist. The Holy Spirit alone is Jesus' representative, indwelling Jesus' disciples.

The Holy Spirit is the full expression of God the Father and God the Son. Jesus said the Spirit would enable us to become more like Him (see John 14:10-14,19-20,26; 15:4-17; 16:8, 13-15). The Spirit is the fullness of God's character, love, presence, plan, and purpose.

As the Spirit does His work, He transforms us into the image of Christ Jesus. The process of spiritual transformation brings tremendous healing to the person who previously had been ripped apart by sin. Only the Holy Spirit can renew our minds and bring us to the wholeness of spiritual transformation.

Will you stop for a moment and thank God for the gift of His Holy Spirit? Then depend on the indwelling Spirit to work in you and through you as you go about your day's activities.

———◆———

Lord, because of Your great love, I am being transformed into Your likeness "with ever-increasing glory, which comes from the Lord, who is the Spirit." 2 Corinthians 3:18

"God has poured out his love into our hearts by the Holy Spirit, whom he has given us." Romans 5:5

Thank You for the gift of Your Spirit. Please help me to depend on Your Spirit to work in my life today.

THE FILLING
OF THE HOLY SPIRIT

When we accept the sacrifice of Jesus for the remission of our sins, and seek the forgiveness that He made possible through His death on the cross, we receive the Holy Spirit. At that moment, the Spirit of God seals us (see 2 Corinthians 1:22; Ephesians 1:13; 4:30). The Holy Spirit guarantees that our status as God's own will never change. Because His seal is secure, our salvation is sure.

While the sealing of the Holy Spirit occurs only once—at the time of our surrender to Him—the filling of our lives with God's Spirit is something that can and should happen continuously. This filling is dependent upon our response to God's gracious gift of salvation and our desire to obey Jesus as our Lord. As we are filled, God's Spirit guides us, admonishes us, corrects us, comforts us, and leads us away from evil and toward the good plans and purposes of God.

While every Christian is sealed by the Holy Spirit, not every Christian chooses to be continuously filled by the Spirit. God waits for us to open ourselves to Him and yield our will to His will. It is our responsibility and privilege to invite the Holy Spirit to do His work in us and through us every day.

When the apostle Paul wrote, "Be filled with the Spirit" (Ephesians 5:18), he used a Greek verb tense that means "to be constantly or continually filled." We live in the healing power of the Holy Spirit when we are continually filled with Him.

Let me be very clear on one aspect of the Spirit's filling. At the time of salvation, a person receives the whole of the person of the Holy Spirit, not just part of Him. But allowing Him to control our words, actions, and decisions is a daily process. We must submit every part of our lives, every day, to the Spirit's control. Have you yielded all of your life to the working of the Holy Spirit, or have you cornered His presence and power into one small area of your life?

Why don't you take time today to confess and expose the areas in your life in which you have shut the Holy Spirit out? Why don't you open that room in your heart to His healing power? Let Him break down the stronghold that is keeping you a prisoner. Then give praise to God for Jesus who made it possible for God's Spirit to dwell within you.

———◆———

Lord, thank You for sending Your Holy Spirit, who has sealed me and who binds me to You: "We know that we live in him and he in us, because he has given us of his Spirit." 1 John 4:13

O God, I thank You for the security I enjoy through Your Spirit. He "set his seal of ownership on us, and put his Spirit in our hearts as a deposit, guaranteeing what is to come." 2 Corinthians 1:22

Thank You, Jesus, for promising us a Comforter to dwell within us: "The Holy Spirit, whom the Father will send in my name, will teach you all things and will remind you of everything I have said to you." John 14:26

Help me today, Father, to open my entire life to the control of Your Spirit.

THE POWER OF THE SPIRIT

❁

When we speak of the power of the Holy Spirit, many people—even Christians—misunderstand the meaning of *power*. They tend to define power as the world defines it.

In the world's view, power conveys the ability to control people, events, and circumstances for our own advantage. In the world, power brings independence and self-sufficiency, with no need for God's help or the assistance of others.

While many devote their lives to achieving this goal, this type of power can never satisfy the soul or bring joy or peace. The world's power is temporary, leaving a person always wanting more.

In describing the power of the Holy Spirit, the Bible paints quite a different picture (see Luke 24:49; Acts 1:8; 2 Corinthians 12:9). The word translated as "power" in the English Bible is the Greek word *dynamis,* from which we get the word *dynamite.* In

Acts 1:8, Jesus told His disciples that before they would be able to evangelize the world, they must receive the *dynamis* of the Holy Spirit.

The Holy Spirit possesses a dynamite-like power that works within a believer to blast out anything that is unlike God. It is not a power that exalts one person above others. It does not manipulate or control others. Instead, the Holy Spirit uses His power to break us so that He might remake us. The more we get self out of the way and yield our will to His, the more powerfully He is able to pour Himself through us to others, and the more powerfully He is able to transform our lives. We are merely the conduits, the channels that God's power moves through.

The Holy Spirit empowers us to be witnesses of God's love, to live in a way that pleases God, to meet fully the demands and pressures of life, and to resist temptation. The power of the Holy Spirit is the only power that is sufficient to win spiritual battles against our own selfish desires and the minions of Satan.

Set aside some time today to ask God to free you from the desire to control others and to lead you to become a clean vessel that can be used to transmit His power. Ask Him to do the same for your spouse, your children, your coworkers, and friends.

———◆———

Lord, teach me about the true power of Your Spirit and the willingness to submit to His power: "My message and my preaching were not with wise and persuasive words, but with a demonstration of the Spirit's power." 1 Corinthians 2:4

I confess that You alone are God. Please display Your power in and through my life today. Make me a clean and willing vessel.

KNOWING THE SPIRIT'S POWER

❦

If God's awesome power is available to us through the Holy Spirit, how can we tap into it? The answer is clear: We must acknowledge our utter helplessness and our complete dependence on God. The Bible tells us that God shows Himself strongest in the most humble of hearts. God is able to meet every need in the life that is broken in surrender and worship of Him alone.

We put ourselves in position to receive God's power when we become realistic about our limitations. The key to spiritual power is humility, not striving for success and seeking to promote ourselves. Whenever I am tempted to believe that I'm responsible for some breakthrough in our ministry, I remember the many times I have felt overwhelmed by the demands and the difficulty of living for God. When I recall my helplessness, I grow closer to God, the Source of my strength.

As a pastor I often find myself crying, "Lord, help me. Lord, enable me. Lord, give me your power!" I want the power of the Lord so I can witness with boldness and effectiveness. I want His power so I can live in a way that is fully pleasing to Him. I want God's power to make me equal to the demands and pressures I face and to give me victory over sin. I want God's power working in my life to defeat the spiritual enemy who seeks to bring about loss, destruction, and an end to blessing in my life (see John 10:10).

If we rely on our own strength, we will surely be defeated. But in the strength of the Holy Spirit, we are in position to be more than conquerors over everything that confronts us (see Romans 8:37).

Are you tempted to take matters into your own hands and rely on your own skills and resourcefulness? Take time today to admit your inadequacies and confess your past attempts to lean on your own strength rather than rely on the power of God's Spirit.

———◆———

Lord, empower me afresh with Your Holy Spirit so that I might be equal to the challenges of this day: "But you will receive power when the Holy Spirit comes on you; and you will be my witnesses." Acts 1:8

I confess my inadequacies and my tendency to rely on my own abilities: " 'Not by might nor by power, but by my Spirit,' says the LORD Almighty." Zechariah 4:6

DON'T QUENCH THE SPIRIT

In the middle of summer, it's difficult to resist the appeal of a soft drink commercial on television. No matter what brand it is, the beverage maker promises that drinking an ice-cold glass of his soda will quench our summer thirst. We all know that a cold drink on a hot day will not make our thirst disappear forever, but will in fact suppress it for the moment.

The common English usage of the word *quench* might confuse us when we read Scripture warning us not to quench the Spirit of God. The Greek word that is translated as "quench" means "to extinguish." This word has a stronger meaning than "temporary suppression." It means "to extinguish, snuff out, or put an end to." A modern English translation says, "Do not put out the Spirit's fire" (1 Thessalonians 5:19). The same word can be used to describe the snuffing out of a candle.

This does not mean that we can permanently remove the

Holy Spirit from our lives. The Spirit is indestructible in His Person and inextinguishable in His strength. Rather, quenching the Spirit means we can resist something the Holy Spirit wants to do in us or through us. It is refusing to follow His leading, ignoring His warnings and charging ahead to do things our way and in our own timing.

We all come to crossroads where we have the opportunity to yield to the Holy Spirit or to quench the Spirit's work. We may sense that we are to serve in some way, to give money to meet a need, or to change a destructive habit. To quench the Spirit is to say no to the Lord in these moments and to choose instead to pursue our own personal goals. Just as it is possible to disobey God even when His will for us is abundantly clear, it is also possible for us to live in such a way that the Holy Spirit withholds His power from our lives.

Have you lost the power of God by putting out the Holy Spirit's fire? Today you can repent and ask God to forgive you. Then commit your day to Him. Ask God to help you obey the gentle voice of the Holy Spirit. Ask Him to renew His power and work within you.

Dear Father, I know that You tell us in Your Word, "Do not put out the Spirit's fire" and "do not grieve the Holy Spirit of God, with whom you were sealed for the day of redemption." 1 Thessalonians 5:19; Ephesians 4:30

Today I ask You, O Lord, to guide me as You have promised: "Whether you turn to the right or to the left, your ears will hear a voice behind you, saying, 'This is the way; walk in it.'" Isaiah 30:21

Help me today to obey that gentle voice.

THE FRUIT OF THE HOLY SPIRIT

If you have ever watched the harvesting of grapes, you know that two people usually work together. One person holds an open basket while the other cuts the grapes and lays the clusters into the container. As long as the basket carrier keeps the basket open and follows closely along with the cutter, her fruit basket will soon be filled to overflowing. But if she closes the basket or lags behind, she can't receive the fruit.

In a similar way, as long as you walk closely with the Lord and keep your life open to receive the daily filling of the Holy Spirit, your life will be filled with the fruit of the Spirit. The fruit of the Spirit is character rather than conduct; it is *being* rather than *doing*. Many people mistakenly refer to the "fruits" of the Spirit. However, the fruit of the Spirit is a single fruit, not an assortment. It is the whole of God's nature imparted to us and flowing out of us as evidence that the Spirit resides in us. God's nature is not fragmented. We cannot receive just one aspect of His being. We bear *all* the fruit of the Spirit, not *some* fruit.

The apostle Paul summarized the composite nature of God's character as "love, joy, peace, patience, kindness, goodness, faithfulness, gentleness [meekness] and self-control" (Galatians 5:22-23). This also describes the fruit that the Holy Spirit bears in our lives.

We cannot talk ourselves into developing these character traits. We cannot study our way into them. They are the by-product of our allowing the Spirit to do His work in us as we abide in the words of Christ Jesus, obey the commands of Christ, and follow the leading of the Holy Spirit. Jesus commands us to stay connected to Him, to abide in Him, to rely upon Him, and to turn to Him when facing every decision. Abiding involves becoming so connected to Him that we no longer can tell where our will ends and His begins.

When we experience the moment-by-moment filling of God's Spirit, we begin to bear the fruit of the Spirit. That's when we start to manifest the outworking of the Holy Spirit's presence. His work will transform our thoughts and emotions as well as our behavior toward others.

Will you ask the Lord today to keep you connected to the Vine? If you feel that your connection has been broken, ask Him to restore you and to make you fruitful today.

———◆———

Lord Jesus, help me always to walk closely behind You so that I can manifest Your character through the fruit of Your Spirit: "But the fruit of the Spirit is love, joy, peace, patience, kindness, goodness, faithfulness, gentleness and self-control. Against such things there is no law." Galatians 5:22-23

I want to abide always in You and have You abide in me: "If a man remains in me and I in him, he will bear much fruit; apart from me you can do nothing." John 15:5

PART II

THE HEALING WORK OF GOD'S LOVE, JOY, AND PEACE

The mind controlled by the Spirit
is life and peace.

ROMANS 8:6

GOD LOVES US. PERIOD.

❀

We all are starving for a personal experience of genuine, biblical love. The teachers of shadow spirituality tell us that it is only as we love ourselves that we are able to open our hearts to receive divine love. But this is the opposite of God's true spirituality. We come to Christ when we recognize that we are *nothing* without God and that, even in our sinful state, Christ died for us. The person who is absorbed with self-love can't find God because he sees no need for God.

True love does not occur apart from God, and for the follower of Christ, love is not optional. That is because God's love flows from His nature. As John wrote, "God is love" (1 John 4:8). His character is defined by love. God has made an eternal choice from the foundation of all creation that He will love His creation.

At no time does God say, "I love you whenever it's convenient. I love you when you are good. I love you as long as you promise to try harder." God's love is constant. It is sacrificial, aimed always at bringing about our eternal good.

God's love never varies. He loves us even when we are rebellious and disobedient, when we turn our backs on Him and refuse to return His love. He loves us. Period. He loves us because that is God's choice. God *is* love.

Jesus said in the most famous verse of the New Testament, "For God so loved the world that he gave his one and only Son, that whoever believes in him shall not perish but have eternal life" (John 3:16). There's nothing in that statement about our earning or being worthy of God's love. All the motivation and impetus are on God's part.

Our appreciation for God's love will grow when we realize that His love is not artificial or cheap. When God said to humankind, "I love you," He gave up all that was most precious to Him. He said "I love you" by paying the price for our sin, and that price was the death of His own Son.

Take a moment and allow yourself to be overwhelmed with the unconditional love of God. Praise Him for loving you even when you were at odds with Him.

———◆———

God, You truly are Love, and we are able to love You and others "because [You] first loved us." 1 John 4:19

You are faithful, Lord, "keeping [Your] covenant of love to a thousand generations of those who love [You] and keep [Your] commands." Deuteronomy 7:9

I know Your love will never fail or even diminish. Thank You, dear Father, for Your constant love for me.

THE SPIRIT REVEALS GOD'S LOVE

❀

We would be blind to God's awesome, unlimited, undeserved love if it weren't for the witness of the Holy Spirit. The Holy Spirit reveals that God's love was extended to us first, even when we were unworthy. The Holy Spirit also shows us that God does not require us to clean up our sinful lives before He will love us. Rather, God sent His Son to die on our behalf when we were still in full rebellion against Him (see Romans 5:6-8).

Many years ago the Holy Spirit revealed to me that I was being controlled by a life of sin. I was living under the horrors of spiritual slavery. The Holy Spirit said to me, "I can free you! Do you want to be freed?"

At first I was reluctant to turn from my old way of life. *If I break free of this bondage,* I reasoned, *I might miss out on the good things that I can get from my slave master.*

Here is what the Holy Spirit showed me: "Your slave master [Satan] tells you lies so that you will believe that he always will have you under his control." Then the Holy Spirit asked me, "Is that what you want?"

My answer was a resounding no!

Then God's Spirit graciously said, "Let me introduce you to Jesus. He has already rendered Satan ineffective. Jesus loves you with immeasurable, incomprehensible, unconditional love. He died for you even when you preferred to hang out with your slave master, and now He invites you to experience all the riches that He has in store for you."

The Holy Spirit showed me through the eyes of faith what my future with this loving Savior would be like. He opened my eyes to the glories, joys, and blessedness of heaven. By this time I was crying out, "Save me from my slave master! Release me from my sin and guilt and bondage." And in Jesus' great love, He did just that.

God's love drives Him to seek us out. His love always motivates Him toward us with the purpose of forgiving us, restoring us, and showering His mercy and grace upon us. This is the healing and wholeness of God's love toward us.

Have you truly experienced God's love? Perhaps you have turned away from Him and forgotten the joy of His embrace. Reach out to Him today and open your heart to receive His overflowing, healing love.

———◆———

Lord, help me let go of my selfish agenda and open myself fully to Your love: "And hope does not disappoint us, because God has poured out his love into our hearts by the Holy Spirit, whom he has given us." Romans 5:5

Help me, Father, to trust in Your compelling love for me: "I, the LORD, have called you in righteousness; I will take hold of your hand. I will keep you and will make you to be a covenant for the people and a light for the Gentiles, to open eyes that are blind, to free captives from prison and to release from the dungeon those who sit in darkness." Isaiah 42:6-7

THE HEALING POWER
OF GOD'S LOVE

The Bible explains that God's love binds up all our emotional, mental, and spiritual wounds—and it binds up our broken relationships. But how?

Love restores us to the Father, rebuilding us from the inside out. It refashions the way we see ourselves: We are lovable because God has made us the object of His love. We are capable of loving others because God now loves others through us.

In any area in which we feel unworthy, God's love conveys, "I made you, I redeemed you, and I want you with Me forever!"

In any area in which we feel rejected, God's love says, "I have adopted you. Come, talk to Me and spend time with Me."

In any area in which we feel shame over our sin, God's love says, "The moment you confessed and repented is the moment I forgave you. You are free of shame because of My mercy. Go and sin no more."

God's love is compelling, but He does not force us to accept it. He waits for our response. We must be ready to accept the love that He longs to shower on us through His Spirit.

As long as we are relying on our own strength to get through life, we won't recognize our need for the comfort of God's love. But when we feel deep remorse over our sin and our failure to trust in God, that's when we realize our need for the forgiving mercy of God's love. Sin keeps us from God's love, but seeking God's forgiveness restores us to Him.

As you rest in God's forgiveness, don't allow the sin of unforgiveness to keep you estranged from another person. Reach out to that person with forgiveness and love. Not only will you be healed in the process, but others will find themselves in position to be healed as well. Let the healing power of God's love restore your own life, and allow God to use you to bring His healing love to others.

Do you need to experience God's forgiveness? Is there someone that you need to forgive? Ask God to reveal the healing power of His love to you. You can forgive others because He has forgiven you.

———◆———

On this day, I pray to You, "Have mercy on me, O God, according to your unfailing love; according to your great compassion blot out my transgressions." Because of Your mercy, I will "trust in your unfailing love; my heart rejoices in your salvation." "Praise be to God, who has not rejected my prayer or withheld his love from me!" Psalms 51:1; 13:5; 66:20

Thank You, Father, for the healing that comes through Your unfailing love.

THE JOY OF THE LORD

Years ago someone noted that the best argument for Christianity is a Christian who is joyful, certain of his faith, and complete in his character. Likewise, one of the strongest arguments *against* Christianity is a believer who is somber and joyless, self-righteous and smug, feeling complacent in his consecrated state.

Joy—mentioned seventy times in the New Testament—is essential to the Christian life. Yet as much as we value joy, many of us fail to connect our faith with God's joy. Some Christians even think that Sunday morning is a time to be somber. My friend, take this to heart: True spirituality finds true expression in the joy of the Lord!

The problem is that the world's obsession with happiness is

often confused with spiritual joy. The world may speak about joy while thinking about candy (Almond Joy), a computer game accessory (joystick), or going for an unauthorized trip in a fast car (joyride). But each of these is nothing more than a moment of temporary, fleeting pleasure.

One of the main distinctions between joy and happiness is that joy is an abiding quality while happiness is a temporary emotion. Happiness is rooted in favorable circumstances and enjoyable activities. Because it is dependent on external conditions, happiness can never be fully satisfied.

True spiritual joy comes from the inside. It does not come from favorable economic conditions, being accepted by society, or owning a luxury car. Joy comes from one thing only: a sure knowledge that you are saved through the death and the resurrection of the Lord Jesus Christ. Real joy comes from knowing that your sins are forgiven, that God is working all things together for your eternal good, and that He is preparing an eternal home for you.

Jesus said, "Remain in my love…that your joy may be complete" (John 15:10-11). As we abide in the knowledge that Jesus is our Savior and the Lord of our lives, the Holy Spirit is free to manifest the character trait of joy in our lives.

You can experience the joy of the Lord afresh today by abiding in the amazing love of Jesus. Ask your heavenly Father to replace your desire for temporary feelings of happiness with His lasting joy.

Dear Lord, I want to know Your joy more than the fleeting pleasure of happiness: "The precepts of the LORD are right, giving joy to the heart. The commands of the LORD are radiant, giving light to the eyes." Psalm 19:8

Help me abide in Your sure promise: "You have made known to me the path of life; you will fill me with joy in your presence." Psalm 16:11

JOY DEFEATS ENVY

❁

If you want to maintain the joy of the Holy Spirit, be on guard against the sin of envy. Envy and jealousy are works of the flesh that wage war against the spirit and destroy your joy (see Galatians 5:17,19-21). In order to protect your joy, you must learn to recognize envy and jealousy.

Jealousy is a passionate desire to hold on to something that is already yours. The Lord God is described as being "jealous" for His people—He desires to keep them close to Himself. This is the legitimate, protective feeling the Lord has regarding something that rightfully belongs to Him.

On a human scale, however, jealousy can consume us. Extremely jealous people experience a great deal of anxiety as they try to cling tightly to everything in an attempt to prevent others from winning away what they feel is rightfully theirs.

Envy is a bit different. Many people who seem to have

everything still envy the possessions of others. Envy is the desire to have more than you already have, and it will incapacitate you. Proverbs 14:30 says, "A heart at peace gives life to the body, but envy rots the bones."

The apostle Paul found the solution to bone-rotting envy: the healing that comes only through contentment. He wrote,

> I have learned to be content whatever the circumstances.
> I know what it is to be in need, and I know what it is
> to have plenty. I have learned the secret of being content
> in any and every situation, whether well fed or hungry,
> whether living in plenty or in want. (Philippians 4:11-12)

In the end, both envy and jealousy involve a preoccupation with what we want to control or possess. They cause us to doubt God's sufficiency and His love, and they eat away at our joy. The joy of God's Spirit does not coexist with jealousy or envy.

Examine your heart carefully. Are you harboring feelings of envy or jealousy? If so, confess these destructive thoughts to the Lord. With envy and jealousy regularly removed from your heart, you will be free to experience the power and blessing of God's joy.

———◆———

Lord, let Your joy and Your love rule in my heart to defeat all envy and jealousy: "Love is patient, love is kind. It does not envy, it does not boast, it is not proud." 1 Corinthians 13:4

Your Word instructs us, "Rid yourselves of all malice and all deceit, hypocrisy, envy, and slander of every kind. Like newborn babies, crave pure spiritual milk, so that by it you may grow up in your salvation, now that you have tasted that the Lord is good." 1 Peter 2:1-3

Lord, I can be content because I know that You alone are good and that I truly lack nothing.

THE HEALING POWER
OF GOD'S JOY

The best way to experience the joy of the Holy Spirit is to stop what you are doing and park yourself in God's parking lot. Sit quietly and allow your mind and heart to rest in His sufficiency while the Lord assures you afresh that you are the recipient of His grace and mercy, not only today, but always.

To truly benefit from the healing power of joy, we must understand four important truths:

Joy is not the absence of adversity. Joy flourishes in the lives of those who pursue true spirituality even in the face of trouble. From a prison cell, Paul wrote to the Philippians, "Rejoice in the Lord always. I will say it again: Rejoice!" (Philippians 4:4).

Joy is not the absence of pain or sorrow. Rather, joy is rooted in the sure knowledge that God is with us in our pain and sorrow and that absolutely nothing can separate us from His love (see Romans 8:38-39). God is at work on our behalf whether we are employed or unemployed, embraced or rejected by others, criticized or praised.

Joy is not the denial of reality. Some people believe that joy in the midst of pain and sorrow is nothing more than a refusal to acknowledge the reality of difficulties. God's Word never requires us to deny reality; rather, we are to confront reality with faith, live above the moment, and see the future that God holds out to us.

Joy is not based on having things under control. Countless people believe they will have joy if they can just get past the current crisis, pay their current bills, meet the current deadlines. These expectations are doomed to failure because joy is not the result of our striving. Joy is the result of *letting go* of anxiety and trusting God to do His work in us and on our behalf.

Your joy will come as a result of trusting God to walk with you through the difficult times as He works behind the scenes to bring about blessing. The joy of the Lord gives you strength and heals you.

Have you wasted weeks, or even months, striving to gain control in your life? Have you agonized during times of trial or uncertainty, trying to fix the situation? Take a moment to sit in silence before the Lord to allow the healing power of His joy to wash over you.

———◆———

Dear Father, I know that I am powerless to control the difficulties in my life. You are the only One who has such power: "The LORD has done great things for us, and we are filled with joy." Psalm 126:3

Help me put an end to worry by trusting in You: "When anxiety was great within me, your consolation brought joy to my soul." Psalm 94:19

Lord, this is my prayer today: "Satisfy us in the morning with your unfailing love, that we may sing for joy and be glad all our days." Psalm 90:14

OUR HUNGER FOR PEACE

❀

"Peace I leave with you; my peace I give you. I do not give to you as the world gives. Do not let your hearts be troubled and do not be afraid" (John 14:27). That is how Jesus described the root causes of worry and anxiety, which for all of us are fear and a troubled heart.

How do our hearts become troubled? Sin interrupts our peace by causing shame and worry. Or we are injured by another's sinful behavior, causing us to feel pain, powerlessness, and anger. The result for both the sinner and the sinned-against is a loss of peace.

In addition to the troubling words or actions of others, we can grow anxious over an encounter with the general sinfulness of humankind. Through the ages, our fallen human condition has resulted in a corruption of the earth, producing pollution and incurable illnesses that threaten our well-being.

But anxiety also arises from far less serious life issues. Anxiety

—a close cousin of fear—is a preoccupation with unimportant things. This preoccupation is often accompanied by false reasoning that if things were resolved, life would be great. We tell ourselves, *If I only had X number of dollars in the bank, then I could stop worrying.* The truth is just the opposite: Financial security is powerless to deliver peace of mind because earthly riches are temporary.

God grants genuine peace only on the basis of righteousness, which results from our having His righteousness working within us. And that emanates from a right relationship with God through the sacrifice of His Son. In Christ, our future is secure—both on earth and in eternity. This is the spiritual truth that calms anxiety in our hearts.

What is your anxiety level? Are you suppressing feelings of worry or dread? The peace God offers is more powerful than all of your emotions. Ask Him to show you the amazing benefits of living under the shelter of His peace.

———

Lord, I continue to worry over things I can't control. I want to hand my concerns over to You today so I can find shelter in Your incredible peace. Help me trust You. I want to enjoy the confidence and security of Your peace: "The LORD gives strength to his people; the LORD blesses his people with peace." Therefore, "turn from evil and do good; seek peace and pursue it." Psalms 29:11; 34:14

GOD'S PEACE BANISHES FEAR

Every time I read about a biblical character who lacked peace, I see fear. And every time I see fear, I notice that faith is lacking. Fear is the great foe of peace, and it comes in many guises, including panic, dread, and worry. Getting to the core of the fear that lies behind many other emotions can be like peeling layers of old wallpaper. You recognize regret, and underneath it you uncover self-centeredness. You peel back self-centeredness, and you find doubt. You peel back doubt, and you find fear. Fear, ultimately, is a lack of trust in God.

We struggle with a fear of failure, of sickness, of a bad outcome for our children. In some cases, it's a nagging fear that cannot be readily defined. And at times, fear actually brings about the thing we fear most. We fear rejection, so we avoid taking the risk of reaching out to others. We then become isolated, which causes us to appear arrogant, so that others begin to avoid us.

Thus our fear brings about the rejection that we feared at the outset.

Anytime we allow a problem to loom larger than God, we are prone to fear. The greater our fear grows, the less we are able to see God beyond the problem. The solution is not to deny or run away from the problem, but to run to the Source of peace. In the middle of the storm, run to the place of utmost safety. Take your mind off the problem by focusing on God. Meditate on His goodness and His greatness. Fear is self-focused, but peace comes through centering our minds and hearts on who God is.

Isaiah 43 begins, "Fear not, for I have redeemed you; I have summoned you by name; you are mine" (verse 1). Faith in our heavenly Father replaces the anxiety of our what-if questions with great assurance. God is in control of *all* things, including every detail and circumstance of our lives and our deaths. Therefore, we can rest in that knowledge and experience His peace.

What are you most afraid of—failure, loss, potential tragedy? No matter what it is, you can be certain that Jesus conquered all of these things at the Cross. Ask Him to fill your heart and calm your mind with His supernatural peace.

———◆———

Lord, I submit my fear to you at this moment: "I will lie down and sleep in peace, for you alone, O LORD, make me dwell in safety." Psalm 4:8

In faith, I claim Your promise to me: "Peace I leave with you; my peace I give you.... Do not let your hearts be troubled and do not be afraid." John 14:27

I know that You, Lord, are bigger than anything that troubles me: "Though the mountains be shaken and the hills be removed, yet my unfailing love for you will not be shaken nor my covenant of peace be removed." Isaiah 54:10

THE HEALING POWER
OF GOD'S PEACE

❀

Our faith is activated when we say to Jesus, "I know You are the answer to all of my needs and the solution to all of my problems. I believe—help any unbelief that remains in me to be turned into belief." This is the path to God's peace amid the troubles of life.

Faith opens us up to "God possibilities." God can do all things, and He will open a way where there seems to be no way. Faith causes us to cling to God's promise that a bright future lies ahead. And even if that future is not experienced on earth, it most assuredly will be experienced in heaven.

Faith is the direct path to God's healing peace, which comes to us in "radiant circles." First, we experience the peace of God in our hearts and minds. Our emotions and our spirits are settled, at rest—regardless of the turmoil raging around us. As our minds and hearts become calm, we are more open to God's wisdom. That is when a clearer awareness of our problems emerges.

A second realm of peace has to do with our outward behavior. The person who feels God's peace cannot help but act in a way that reflects the peace of God. What is inside the person manifests itself in body language, expression, speech, and other forms of behavior toward others. Then as the circles of peace radiate outward, those who follow God will resolve their problems with the peace of God reigning in their hearts. When others observe this, they very often seek to align themselves with these peaceful problem-solvers who follow the God of peace. God's peace, active in our lives, draws others to God.

The Bible teaches us, "Whoever would love life and see good days...must seek peace and pursue it" (1 Peter 3:10-11). In choosing to trust God with our problems, we are putting ourselves into a position for the Holy Spirit to heal us by filling our lives with His peace. God's peace encompasses all of life, restoring us and bringing us to wholeness. We enjoy the healing work of peace in our lives as we extend the healing power of peace to others.

Will you allow God to renew your trust in Him? Will you allow His perfect peace to free your mind from all that troubles you? No matter what you are facing, put your trust in God and invite His peace to wash over you. Then give praise to Jesus, the Prince of Peace.

———◆———

Lord, You know the things that steal my peace. Please give me the faith to trust You in every circumstance: "You will keep in perfect peace him whose mind is steadfast, because he trusts in you." For "the mind set on the flesh is death, but the mind set on the Spirit is life and peace." Isaiah 26:3; Romans 8:6 (NASB)

PART III

THE HEALING WORK
OF GOD'S PATIENCE,
KINDNESS, AND GOODNESS

How great is your goodness,
which you have stored up for those who fear you,
which you bestow in the sight of men
on those who take refuge in you.

PSALM 31:19

THE KEY TO WAITING

❀

Not long ago I went to a bookstore to find a book on patience, but I came away empty-handed. Patience is something most people want, but it's not a popular book topic! Very few of us can develop and then maintain patience. Even Christians want instant answers to prayer, quick holiness, ready-made spiritual maturity, and miracles on demand.

I admit that I'm no expert on patience. I have to remind myself that God took six months to reveal to Noah the best parking place for the ark! If you struggle with patience as I do, look with me at the most common causes of a lack of patience.

A narrow worldview. Sometimes a person focuses only on his own needs and his own little world. Impatience is manifested when his needs go unmet, his schedule is interrupted, or his views are challenged.

A need for visible evidence. We become impatient when we

insist on concrete proof that things are improving. We forget that God is always at work on our behalf, even when we don't sense that things are going the way we want them to. True spirituality produces patience that springs from the expectancy that God cares about every detail of our lives, with or without visible evidence.

Unrealistic expectations. Impatience arises when we expect others to function just as we do. We need to develop realistic expectations, allowing others the freedom to be who God made them to be.

Out-of-balance priorities. When we make the wrong things high priorities, we become impatient. When God is at the center of our lives, however, our priorities will fall into place, and we'll find greater patience with any life circumstance. The patient person continues in faith until God accomplishes His will in him and through him.

The Lord sent His Holy Spirit to comfort you at all times—including the times of waiting. Begin to praise God for His infinite, intricate care for you. Though for a while God may be silent, His Spirit is always with you, and an answer will come in His perfect timing.

———◆———

Lord, let me rest in the calm assurance that You are constantly at work on my behalf: "Yet those who wait for the LORD will gain new strength; they will mount up with wings like eagles, they will run and not get tired, they will walk and not become weary." Isaiah 40:31 (NASB)

Lord, let me wait patiently for Your answers: "Be still before the LORD and wait patiently for him; do not fret when men succeed in their ways, when they carry out their wicked schemes." Psalm 37:7

THE ENEMY OF PATIENCE

❖

Impatience is marked by many emotions. Chief among them are frustration and feelings of being frantic or out of control. At the root of impatience, however, is anger.

The Greek word that is translated as "patience," *makrothumia,* is made up of two words. The first half of the Greek word means "anger," which includes frustration. The second half means either "long in coming" or "slow in appearing." Patience, then, is anger that is delayed and frustration that is long postponed.

The Lord describes Himself as being slow to anger. He revealed His nature to Moses, saying, "The LORD, the LORD, the compassionate and gracious God, slow to anger, abounding in love and faithfulness, maintaining love to thousands, and forgiving wickedness, rebellion and sin" (Exodus 34:6-7).

The opposite of patience is a quickness to become angry. When someone speaks to us rudely or cuts us off in traffic, we experience an outburst of spontaneous anger or a quick eruption of frustration. An equally unhealthy response would be to suppress our feelings of anger. This anger is stone-faced and silent. But suppressed anger doesn't disappear, it just goes underground where it can fester and one day erupt like a volcano. Meanwhile, it manifests itself in cold fury and bitter resentment. Holding anger inside brings a hardness of heart and very little flexibility or forgiveness toward others.

True spirituality brings healing both to hotheads and to those who habitually suppress their anger. The solution that God's Spirit brings is the "long in coming" ability to express anger positively and appropriately, which is coupled with the willingness to allow God's patience to work in and through us.

Take time to ask the One who is slow to anger to teach you how to be patient in everyday life. Praise God for His amazing character. Thank Him for His patience with you, for withholding His wrath and sending His Son to die for your sins.

———◆———

Lord, I praise and worship You because You are "slow to anger, abounding in love and forgiving sin and rebellion." Numbers 14:18

In Your Word You instruct us, "In your anger do not sin," and "Turn from wrath; do not fret—it leads only to evil. For evil men will be cut off, but those who hope in the LORD will inherit the land." Psalms 4:4; 37:8-9

SPIRIT-PRODUCED PATIENCE

We glorify God when we are long-suffering toward those who wrong us. We glorify Him when we are long-suffering in our actions to confront sin and evil and when we are patient but steadfast in our refusal to give in to temptation. It is then that we are manifesting the spiritual fruit of patience.

When we don't see an immediate turnaround from evil to good, yet we persevere in standing up for God's righteousness, we are demonstrating the fruit of the Spirit. When everyone around us is taking shortcuts, and we choose instead to do the right thing, we are manifesting the fruit of the Spirit.

But there is no way we can generate this kind of long-suffering spirit apart from the Spirit of God. It is not within our capacity to be this patient. It is when the Spirit of God is pouring patience into our hearts that patience becomes something we *are*, not simply something we *do*. God is patient through us.

Godly patience puts you in a position to do things on God's timetable, based on His deadlines. If God has directed you to perform a certain task or to carry out a particular ministry, then immediately do what God is calling you to do. If you think you don't have the time, then reevaluate the demands that originate with you or with those around you. Those things, in the majority of cases, do not require your immediate attention. But God's leading in your life *does* deserve your immediate compliance.

When we slow down and ask God to fill us with His patience, He will help us see what is truly important. Then we will discover the rhythm of activity that God desires for us and the timetable God has set for us. When we manifest the patience of the Holy Spirit, we become partners in the process of God's revealing Himself to others through us. And in this process, we will find that God is healing our lives day by day.

If you are tired of trying to be patient in your own strength, admit your exhaustion to the Lord. Then allow His Spirit to fill you with His long-suffering patience. With the strength of the Lord, nothing is impossible.

———◆———

Lord, I confess my impatience. Please help me manifest your long-suffering and reject my own self-centered agenda: "And we pray this in order that you may live a life worthy of the

Lord and may please him in every way: bearing fruit in every good work, growing in the knowledge of God, being strengthened with all power according to his glorious might so that you may have great endurance and patience. " Colossians 1:10-11

THE LOST ART OF KINDNESS

Too many people see kindness toward others as a nice option rather than as an essential reflection of the character of God. People show kindness if they happen to be in the right mood, or if being kind can serve their own purposes. But this is not the kindness of the Holy Spirit!

The kindness we read about in the Bible is never determined by convenience or personal preference. It is a vital characteristic of our spirituality because it is a vital characteristic of God's own nature.

God's revelation of Himself to humankind is based on His kindness. It was out of kindness that God made a covenant with Israel, and out of kindness that He kept His side of the covenant despite the blatant disobedience of His people. It was out of kindness that God left the splendor and majesty of heaven and chose to hang on a criminal's cross to pay the wages of sin for all who might believe in Him. It is out of kindness that God accepts repentant sinners.

In a world where shadow spirituality regards self-promotion as a virtue, true spirituality calls us to bear the fruit of kindness. Kindness is a turning of self inside out to give to others, not only of our material resources, but also our time, presence, and attention. Kindness occurs as a by-product of our being filled daily with the Spirit of God and seeking to manifest His life in the world.

The New Age philosophers of shadow spirituality teach their followers to perform acts of kindness in order to feel good about themselves. In sharp contrast, God's true spirituality calls us to take no thought for ourselves but to seek the good of others. We are not to be motivated by the reward that a good deed may bring, but rather by how a good deed might help another person.

Praise God for His kindness! Think of the many wonderful things He has done for you. As you meditate upon His kind Spirit, ask Him to show you how you can demonstrate kindness to another person today.

———◆———

Heavenly Father, you say to your children, "I have loved you with an everlasting love; I have drawn you with loving-kindness." Therefore, Lord, I will tell others of "the kindnesses of the LORD, the deeds for which he is to be praised, according to all the LORD has done for us." Jeremiah 31:3; Isaiah 63:7

THE MARKS OF KINDNESS

❀

Manifesting the kindness of God's Spirit is not a hit-or-miss process of doing nice things. Instead, it is characterized by traits that are clearly defined in the Bible.

First, Spirit-endued kindness gives us the ability to empathize with others by putting ourselves in their place. Too many of us forget what we experienced in an earlier stage of life or during a time of great difficulty. Rigidity and lack of sympathy are by-products of forgetting our own shortcomings. But the kind person has a way of remembering times of struggle and confusion. The kind person can then empathize with others in their weakness or failure. Kindness calls us to reach out to the person who is in bondage to sin and to speak words that bring about repentance and forgiveness.

Second, the person who manifests Spirit-endued kindness can show kindness to himself. This kindness is not self-indulgent but rather merciful. The kind person can let go of his or her past sin and say, "I have been forgiven. I will not beat myself up over sin that God has already forgiven." Instead of punishing himself for his own forgiven sins, the apostle Paul said, "Forgetting what is behind and straining toward what is ahead, I press on toward the goal" of pursuing Christ and of being Christ's witness (Philippians 3:13-14).

Third, the person who manifests Spirit-endued kindness can receive the kind expressions of others. For a number of years this was an area in which I really struggled. I found it easy to show kindness but difficult to accept it from others. Then a friend and mentor said to me, "When you refuse to accept the kindness of others, you are depriving them of the joy of showing kindness." Now I find myself more willing to receive kindness because I want others to experience more of God's joy in their lives!

Fourth, the person who manifests Spirit-endued kindness is willing to let go of hatred, bitterness, and resentment. A person cannot manifest genuine kindness and allow an imaginary war of he-said-I-said and she-did-I-did scenarios to rage in his or her heart.

Only through the power of the Holy Spirit can you show kindness to those who do you wrong. Ask the Lord to empower you to show empathy toward others and mercy toward yourself.

———◆———

Lord, help me empty myself of resentment and bitterness so I can grow in Your kindness and show kindness to others: "For this very reason, make every effort to add to your faith goodness; and to goodness, knowledge; and to knowledge, self-control; and to self-control, perseverance; and to perseverance, godliness; and to godliness, brotherly kindness; and to brotherly kindness, love." 2 Peter 1:5-7

THE HEALING POWER
OF GOD'S KINDNESS

❈

Jesus told a story that opens our eyes to many essential principles about kindness:

> A man was going down from Jerusalem to Jericho, when he fell into the hands of robbers. They stripped him of his clothes, beat him and went away, leaving him half dead.... But a Samaritan, as he traveled, came where the man was; and when he saw him, he took pity on him. He went to him and bandaged his wounds, pouring on oil and wine. Then he put the man on his own donkey, took him to an inn and took care of him. The next day he took out two silver coins and gave them to the innkeeper.

"Look after him," he said, "and when I return, I will
reimburse you for any extra expense you may have."
(Luke 10:30,33-35)

Who was healed in this story? Certainly the man who had
fallen victim to robbers. But by extending this kindness, the
Samaritan also brought about a broader healing. He broke down
certain barriers of prejudice between Samaritans and Jews. Kindness across all boundaries can heal the suspicion and hatred that
build up and eat away at entire groups of people.

God's kindness heals hatred. You cannot show kindness to
a person and continue to hate him. You cannot pray for a person, believing that God will act kindly on his behalf, and continue to resent the person. You cannot extend yourself in giving
to a person and continue to ridicule or feel bitterness toward
that person.

But kindness doesn't stop at healing relationships. It also has
clear personal health benefits. Hatred, bitterness, and resentment
create unease that eats away at the soul. Countless diseases—both
physical and emotional—have been associated with harboring
bitterness.

Kindness opens your soul to the balm of Christ's healing
presence. It makes room for love to take root. So set aside your
own agenda and your fear of rejection and manifest the kindness
of the Holy Spirit. You will bring healing to others and will be
healed yourself in the process.

What type of healing can God's kindness bring to *your* life? Will relationships be restored? Will your emotional or physical health be improved? Ask the Holy Spirit to fill you afresh today, and experience the healing power of God's kindness.

———◆———

Lord, I rejoice in Your kindness. Help me today to "get rid of all bitterness, rage and anger, brawling and slander, along with every form of malice." Lord, help me to be "kind and compassionate to one another, forgiving each other," just as in Your Son You have forgiven me. Ephesians 4:31-32

THE TRUE NATURE
OF GOODNESS

The Greek word for "pure" and "sincere" is *agathos*. This is goodness that springs forth in Christlike actions toward others. *Agathos* is characterized by honesty, truthfulness, and blazing integrity. The goodness of God promotes wholeness in a person's life. Unlike evil, which is fragmented and can work at odds with itself, God's goodness is always unified. It is pervasive, impacting every area of life.

Goodness causes us to orient our lives toward what is good and to focus our thoughts on what is good. The apostle Paul wrote about this to the Philippians: "Whatever is true, whatever is noble, whatever is right, whatever is pure, whatever is lovely, whatever is admirable—if anything is excellent or praiseworthy—

think about such things" (Philippians 4:8). We are to capture our thoughts, turning them toward the goodness of God.

Goodness also changes the way we speak. This does not mean that we simply give up cursing or telling bigoted jokes. Neither is it limited to a commitment to stop gossiping. Certainly, the person who is manifesting the goodness of God's Spirit will not engage in such speech. Good speech, however, goes far beyond the elimination of certain words. Goodness fills our mouths with encouraging words that build up others.

Goodness affects all of our behavior toward others, including our emotional responses. When we respond in anger or bitterness—or when we set out to undercut or defame others—we are taking steps to keep them at a distance, to shut them out of our lives. Jesus taught the opposite approach, the path of goodness:

> Love your enemies, do good to those who hate you...pray for those who mistreat you. If someone strikes you on one cheek, turn to him the other also. If someone takes your cloak, do not stop him from taking your tunic. Give to everyone who asks you, and if anyone takes what belongs to you, do not demand it back. Do to others as you would have them do to you. (Luke 6:27-31)

What a high standard Jesus set! High, but entirely doable in the power of the Holy Spirit.

Are your thoughts, speech, and responses to others governed by the goodness of God's Holy Spirit? As you spend time with the

Lord today, listen to the promptings of His Spirit as He instructs you in the way of goodness.

———◆———

Lord, please open my eyes to the opportunities around me to manifest your goodness toward others in my words, actions, thoughts, and responses: "How great is your goodness, which you have stored up for those who fear you, which you bestow in the sight of men on those who take refuge in you." Psalm 31:19

Lord, I praise You because You have given to us "everything we need for life and godliness" through our knowledge of You, who called us by Your own glory and goodness. 2 Peter 1:3

THE HEALING POWER
OF GOD'S GOODNESS

✿

How can we ever get to the point of loving our enemies, praying for those who mistreat us, and responding with goodness to those who make unreasonable demands on us? We simply can't be that good without God. The path of goodness is closed to us unless He constantly fills us with true spirituality. Here is how the Holy Spirit works in us to accomplish His goodness.

First, the Spirit challenges us to see another person's actions in a new light. The harm that another person commits is not only against us, it is against God as well. Deep inside, the person is most likely reacting against the reflection of God at work in our lives. Others resent our blessings and our character. They hate the fact that we stand up for what they intuitively know to be the truth they have rejected. So they lash out. We must see their behavior as an attempt to lash out at God, not at us.

Then the Holy Spirit leads us to ask, "If this person were to speak to Jesus the way he spoke to me, how would Jesus respond?" We know that Jesus would speak loving words. They may be firm words. They may be words of gentle rebuke, but they would be loving nonetheless. As we seek to emulate Jesus, the Holy Spirit empowers us to do good to a person who has hurt us.

When we do good to those who misuse us, two amazing things happen. First, the other person's hatred is defused. Most people who have willfully caused pain are unsettled by a response of goodness. They are befuddled when a Christian responds with goodness rather than fighting back. Second, the Spirit-led response of goodness touches those who surround the wrongdoer. The actions of goodness lead them to question, "Why are you picking on this person? What purpose is there in pursuing hatred?"

A Christian's goodness provides an opportunity for the Spirit of God to work in another person's life as well as in our own. Thus the spiritual fruit of goodness brings healing to two people.

Do you find it easy to display goodness toward friends but difficult to do likewise toward enemies? You are not alone. Ask God to fill you with goodness so you can do what is impossible without His help.

———◆———

O Lord, give me the power in Your Spirit to be an instrument of Your love and goodness to someone who is unaware of Your saving grace. Help me to never forget Your instructions: "If your enemy is hungry, feed him; if he is thirsty, give him something to drink.... Do not be overcome by evil, but overcome evil with good." Romans 12:20-21

PART IV

THE HEALING WORK
OF GOD'S FAITHFULNESS,
MEEKNESS, AND SELF-CONTROL

Your love, O LORD, reaches to the heavens,
your faithfulness to the skies.

PSALM 36:5

REJOICING IN
GOD'S FAITHFULNESS

George MacDonald, a famous British author of the nineteenth century, once said, "To be trusted is a greater compliment than to be loved."[1] Love is subject to so many emotional interpretations, so many highs and lows, while trust remains steady and constant. It is a positioning of the will and affection that endures.

Alas, trustworthiness is no longer universally held in high esteem. Gone are the days when a promise was a promise, when a person's word was his bond. Likewise, faithfulness has all but fallen out of circulation. The word *faithful* is far more likely to be ascribed to a favorite pet than to a spouse, far more likely to be linked to a geyser than a political leader. And on the rare occasion

---

1. George MacDonald, *The Marquis of Lossie* (1887; reprint, Whitethorn, Calif.: Johannesen, 1995).

when it is associated with a person, it more likely refers to a faithful friend than a faithful God.

But evidence of God's faithfulness is all around us. God always loves. He always forgives repentant sinners. He always accomplishes His plans and fulfills His purposes.

Jesus' disciples knew they could count on Him. Every time they were in danger or need, Jesus was there for them. He came to His disciples with words of comfort and assurance, even if doing so meant walking on water or appearing suddenly inside a locked room. His faithfulness extends even to His walking out of a sealed and heavily guarded tomb.

Just as Jesus can be counted on to keep His word, the Holy Spirit is faithful to us. Jesus said of the Spirit, "He lives with you and will be in you. I will not leave you as orphans; I will come to you" (John 14:17-18). The Holy Spirit is present with us always.

Because God is faithful, we can know for certain that we have the gift of eternal life. We can know that God hears and answers prayer. We can know that God rewards those who earnestly seek Him (see Hebrews 11:6). The person who lives with this kind of assurance has a deep and abiding confidence that cannot be shaken.

How much do you recognize and value God's faithfulness? What price could you place on the assurance you have of God's unchanging love for you? Take time to express your gratitude to Him. Reaffirm your trust in Him and rejoice in the faithfulness of your heavenly Father who will never forget you or turn His back on you.

———◆———

Dear God, today I add my words of praise to the testimony of the prophet Isaiah: "O LORD, you are my God; I will exalt you and praise your name, for in perfect faithfulness you have done marvelous things, things planned long ago." Isaiah 25:1

Lord, I thank You for Your unwavering faithfulness to me: "Your love, O LORD, reaches to the heavens, your faithfulness to the skies." "O LORD God Almighty, who is like you? You are mighty, O LORD, and your faithfulness surrounds you.... Love and faithfulness go before you." Psalms 36:5; 89:8,14

HOW FAITHFULNESS
BRINGS WHOLENESS

Healing is a process—no one is made whole in a day. God works in our lives, molding us bit by bit into the character-likeness of Christ Jesus. The Holy Spirit heals our memories gradually, one relationship or one experience at a time. He deals with us regarding our sins, but again it is one at a time. He addresses our bad habits and our lack of knowledge or understanding, and He does it one issue at a time.

Yet for our healing to continue, we need to join the process by carrying out certain things faithfully and with consistency. It is similar to progress in our physical lives. One day of exercise is not the same as thirty minutes of exercise several times a week.

One day of dieting does not make us thin. It is not what we do some of the time that causes ill health or creates good health—it's what we do most of the time.

The same is true for our spiritual lives. Reading the Bible for an hour once a month isn't as beneficial as reading the Bible ten minutes a day for a month. Praying only when we have a pressing need isn't as beneficial as setting aside time every day to praise, thank, petition, and worship God. Being involved in a ministry once a year doesn't have the same impact on us as being involved on a daily or weekly basis. In all areas of our lives, it's what we do faithfully that produces wholeness.

Faithfulness produces a deep assurance that we are connected to God with a bond that cannot be broken. Faithfulness produces a deep knowledge that what we say and do under the guidance of the Holy Spirit will yield a harvest in God's kingdom. Faithfulness produces a security that manifests itself in confidence and strength of character. Faithfulness is rooted in trust, which is produced when we make a commitment and then honor it, when we say something and mean it. God's faithfulness to us leads to our faithfulness to Him and to others. And ultimately His faithfulness heals us.

If you have been forsaken by a friend, you understand the pain of betrayal. But God can never betray you, which makes your relationship with Him like no other. The closer you draw to Him, the more you will experience the wholeness that comes from trusting in His faithfulness.

———◆———

Lord, on this day and every day after, help me trust in You and in Your faithfulness to me: "Not to us, O LORD, not to us but to your name be the glory, because of your love and faithfulness." Psalm 115:1

O God, let love and faithfulness never leave me; let me bind them around my neck, write them on the tablet of my heart. Proverbs 3:3

DAY 28

MEEKNESS IS NOT WEAKNESS

In the description of the fruit of the Spirit in the New Testament, some Bible versions translate the spiritual fruit of gentleness as "meekness." This is an eye-opening translation of the word if you understand the true meaning of meekness. But both outside the church and within the church, people wrongly think of meekness as weakness or timidity.

Nothing could be further from the truth. The Greek word for "meekness," *praotes,* is synonymous with courage, confidence, security, and strength under control. The Greek philosopher Aristotle had a theory that virtue was held in the balance between two vices. *Praotes,* or meekness, was the virtue that was held in balance between the vice of rage at one extreme and the vice of indifference at the other extreme.

Today we have a phrase, *gentle giant,* that is similar in meaning to the concept of *praotes.* A gentle giant is big, strong, and easily capable of destruction. However, the gentleness of this person causes him to care for the weak, defend the helpless, and nurture the innocent. A gentle giant is strong in character and resolve, yet tender and humble before God.

In the Bible, Moses is described as the meekest man on the face of the earth. In some Bible translations he is called humble (see Numbers 12:3). If you have studied the life of Moses, you know already that he was anything but weak or cowardly. Moses was a strong and decisive leader, and he was completely yielded to God.

The truly meek person stands in humility before God, knowing that all he has, all he does, and all he is, he owes to God. God gives him every heartbeat, every good and productive idea, every opportunity. The meek person knows that he is nothing without God.

At the same time, the meek person knows that because of God, he or she has all things, can do all things, and will accomplish all that God commands him or her to do. The meek person rightly claims that all abilities and success come from God. The meek person lays all accolades at the feet of Jesus and says, "You alone are worthy."

Do you trust God enough to humble yourself before Him? You can come humbly to God without fear of being rejected; instead you will be strengthened by His Spirit. If you are ready to experience God's best for you, make a step of faith toward meekness today.

"Humble yourselves, therefore, under God's mighty hand, that he may lift you up in due time." Lord, I confess that You alone are worthy; all that I have comes from You. I can take credit for no good thing in my life: "A little while, and the wicked will be no more; though you look for them, they will not be found. But the meek will inherit the land and enjoy great peace." 1 Peter 5:6; Psalm 37:10-11

THE HEALING POWER OF GOD'S MEEKNESS

❀

Meekness produces healing and wholeness in us by removing the great stress and burden of self-defense and self-promotion. In their place, meekness brings freedom.

How many people do you know who strive to prove their value to others? They try to build themselves up to win approval or praise. They struggle to elevate themselves to a position where others will think they are important. Let me assure you, all this striving produces stress. It puts us into ongoing competition with other people because in seeking to raise ourselves up, we inevitably put others down. Those who strive for their own success see every other person as a rival.

In sharp contrast, the person who yields all glory and honor to God is freed from a spirit of competition and instead is given a spirit of cooperation. The person who is meek seeks to help others succeed. The meek person wants others to become all that God created them to be. She encourages others to employ their gifts and to use their minds and release their faith. She does not see God's rewards as limited, but rather as unlimited—God's success is for all to enjoy.

The meek person knows that the ultimate work of converting lost souls and transforming believers into Christ's nature is God's work. Therefore, she is freed of all responsibility for transforming or controlling others. The meek person knows that her role is to tell others about Jesus, to obey God's commandments, and to manifest godly fruit. The wooing, winning, saving, healing, and transforming work belongs to God. Only God can deliver a person from evil.

A person who stands humbly before God and others experiences far less stress because he knows that God is in charge. Such a person also has far more friends because he is not trying to control others. Less stress and more friends—that's a combination that promotes emotional, physical, material, and spiritual health. That is the healing work of God's gentle but powerful meekness in our lives.

You'll find freedom in the meekness of God's Holy Spirit—freedom from competition and striving and pride. Decide today to let go of the exhausting cycle of self-defense and self-promotion and to accept the Holy Spirit's meekness.

O God, I want to experience the wholeness that comes through Your meekness. I want all honor and glory to be Yours, not mine: "Let your light shine before men, that they may see your good deeds and praise your Father in heaven." Matthew 5:16

THE MYSTERY
OF SELF-CONTROL

Here is a great mystery involving the way the Holy Spirit works in us: To be self-disciplined, we must yield control of self. The fact is, we all routinely yield control of our lives to forces outside us. We yield to the law of gravity when we trip and fall. We yield the right of way to other motorists in order to avoid an accident. We yield to the wishes of our supervisors at work in order to get our jobs done.

The Holy Spirit calls us to be like Jesus in living a God-ordered life and in remaining totally committed to doing things God's way. We must invite the Holy Spirit to daily fill up our lives. Otherwise, we will be filled with the impulses of the world, the flesh, and the devil. The Spirit calls us to maintain a passion for excellence in serving God and others. And the Holy

Spirit supplies all the power we need to live a disciplined, God-honoring life.

Contrary to the world's beliefs, the spiritual fruit of self-control does not come about through the discipline of self-mastery, but rather through surrendering ourselves to God's control. None of us have the power, capability, or wisdom fully to master our own lives. You cannot resist all the temptations that are hurled at you, control the behavior of those closest to you, or limit the ideas that pop into your mind. You can respond to each of these, but you can never control them.

The self-control of the Holy Spirit is a character trait, not just a daily discipline. Self-control is hearing God say to us, "Speak to that person now" and then going ahead to speak, without asking, "But how will she respond?" Self-control is hearing God say, "Go to a certain place, and when you get there, do this," and then going and doing what He commands, without making any excuses.

Take a moment to surrender control over your goals, your dreams, your frustrations, and your will in exchange for the self-control of the Holy Spirit. God can reveal His plan for your life only when you are fully submitted to Him. Ask God to begin revealing His will to you as you listen with an attentive heart.

———◆———

Lord, I want to live under Your control and to walk in Your way, not according to my own understanding: "Like a city whose walls are broken down is a man who lacks self-control." Therefore, "let us be self-controlled, putting on faith and love as a breastplate, and the hope of salvation as a helmet." Proverbs 25:28; 1 Thessalonians 5:8

Dear Father, help me submit my life to the loving control of Your Holy Spirit.

HOW SELF-CONTROL HEALS US

The spiritual fruit of self-control heals us, in large measure, by bringing order to the chaos of life. When we recognize that God has created us, called us, and equipped us to undertake a specific mission, much of our life comes into focus. We know who we are and what we are to accomplish. We know that the foremost goal God has for us is that we follow Jesus as our Lord.

As we seek to do His will and not our own, we are free to take risks, speak boldly, and face life honestly. As we place our trust in God, we know that He will take everything we do with a sincere heart and turn it into something good within the context of His greater plan and purpose. There is great freedom, comfort, and hope in living this way!

The person who knows that God is in control can relax. He can enjoy the satisfaction of giving his best effort to the accomplishment of God-revealed goals. It might seem obvious, but when we yield control to God, He takes control. He is more than equal to the challenge of making sense of our lives, healing our brokenness, and putting the pieces of our lives into an order that not only makes sense but is beautiful.

When we yield our lives to the daily filling of the Holy Spirit, we give Him an opportunity to show us what needs to be removed from our lives and what we must add. He helps us craft our schedules, new sets of habits, dreams, goals, and plans—all of which combine to produce the person He desires us to become. In yielding control to Him, we become controlled by Him. The more we align ourselves with His commands and His plan, the more we lead a focused, disciplined, and purposeful life. And in this lifelong process, we become whole.

As the Holy Spirit heals us, certainly we are blessed. But the greater benefit goes to those who receive our embrace of compassion and words of encouragement rather than gestures of anger or acts of retribution. As we manifest the fruit of the Holy Spirit, we extend the blessing of God to those around us. This is true spiritual healing.

Trying to control the circumstances of your life will bring only frustration and disappointment. If you are ready to experience the joy and fulfillment of living in the center of God's will, yield complete control of your life to the guidance of His Spirit today. Renew your mind with His promises and begin living in victory!

———◆———

Dear Lord, I want the healing and wholeness that come through yielding to Your control: "Therefore, prepare your minds for action; be self-controlled; set your hope fully on the grace to be given you when Jesus Christ is revealed." 1 Peter 1:13

O God, help me to manifest the spiritual fruit of self-control. I know that through You I can do all things, for You strengthen me. Philippians 4:13